THE SEA GARDEN

A GUIDE TO SEAWEED COOKERY & FORAGING

Marie Power

2013

Reprinted 2018

Published in January 2013.

Original photography, illustration, artwork, design and layout by Emma Power, except where photographs are otherwise credited.
Copyright © Emma Power.
Border graphic on selected pages (from p.29-89) based on photograph of red carrageen seaweed by Dr. Keith Wheeler/Science Photo Library.

Printed in Waterford, Ireland by Intacta Print.

Disclaimer: While every effort has been made to ensure the accuracy of the information presented in this publication, no liability is accepted for any errors or omissions. The information in this book is not intended to replace any advice or treatment given by your medical practitioner.

www.theseagardener.ie

ISBN: 978-0-9575020-0-0

ACKNOWLEDGEMENTS

I would like to thank the following people who provided assistance
in various ways during the production of this book.

Emma Power for creating inspiring drawings and graphics for
The Sea Garden and for photographing the prepared dishes and
seaweeds.

The Dungarvan Museum, the Murray family and the Power-Sheehan
family for photographs.

Stella Whittle (RIP) for tape recording of Pats Burns.

All the people who attended the seaweed workshops along the Co.
Waterford coast since 2007, who tasted food samples and gave
such positive feedback.

My family for their support and encouragement and for always
being available to test the recipes!

*My soul is full of longing
for the secret of the sea,
and the heart of the great ocean
sends a thrilling pulse through me.*

Henry Wadsworth Longfellow, *The Secret of the Sea*, (1850)

This book is for everyone interested in foraging for and using seaweed in their cooking, and will be especially useful if you are a beginner with seaweed. My choice of the Top 10 edible seaweeds on the Irish coast are all here, each with a six-page chapter which describes where and when the species grows, what it looks like and how to cook it. There are two recipes for each seaweed, including sweet and savoury dishes, snacks and one-pot meals, salads, cakes, breads and desserts. Red, green and brown species can be easily found using the colour-coded pages. Quantities given in recipes are for four people (where applicable) and metric measures are used. It may be easier to use a digital kitchen scales, as seaweed weighs very light when dried. There are some recipes using mixed seaweeds and tips on gardening uses. You can use your own foraged seaweed or buy one of the commercially harvested Irish products available. Seaweed is a natural product which varies in texture, size and cooking properties through the seasons.

Pages 20-21 show a scaled chart of all the seaweeds, to help you distinguish them on the basis of size. On pages 22-23, the seaweeds are listed on a simplified shore profile: so that you will know where on the shore to look and what the best foraging season for each species is. Note that the Upper Shore is the higher rock level above low tide mark (not necessarily the rocks closest to the cliff). Plants which can survive longest out of water are higher up on the shore, for example, the wracks, whereas the kelps remain under water almost all the time, and so are found on the Lower Shore.

My approach is to integrate seaweed gradually in the diet, starting with smaller quantities and increasing, so the recipes here tend towards lower quantities. Kelps and wracks contain high levels of iodine and should be limited to 5g dried seaweed a day. Pepper dilisk should only be used as a condiment. If you are undergoing thyroid treatment, consult your medical professional before using seaweed.

I have used organic, locally sourced, quality ingredients as far as possible. Eggs are free-range.

I hope you enjoy trying out these recipes, experimenting with them and finding what works best for you.

LIST OF IMAGES

CONTENTS

CARRAGEEN CHOCOLATE AND LIME PUDDING : p.31
Carrageen

SALMON MOUSSE : p.33
Carrageen

GARDEN & SEA RISOTTO : p.37
Dilisk

BEETROOT & DILISK BREAD : p.39
Dilisk

CARROT CAKE WITH SLEABHCAN : p.43
Sleabhcan

LAVER BREAD : p.45
Sleabhcan

CARAMELISED ONION & GOATS CHEESE TARTS: p.49
Pepper Dilisk

RICE & VEG FRITTATA WITH PEPPER DILISK : p.51
Pepper Dilisk

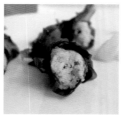
SEA LETTUCE WRAP WITH HUMMUS : p.57
Sea Lettuce

FORAGERS SALAD : p.59
Sea Lettuce

ALARIA AND BRAISED VEGETABLES WITH CRUNCHY
NOODLES : p.63
Alaria

OATY APPLE BOWL WITH ALARIA : p.65
Alaria

TOMATO & BLADDERWRACK SAUCE : p.69
Bladderwrack

ORANGE GINGERCAKE WITH BLADDERWRACK : p.71
Bladderwrack

THAI BEAN & KELP CURRY : p.75
Kelp / Oarweed

SPICED BUTTERNUT SQUASH & APPLE SOUP WITH KELP : p.77
Kelp / Oarweed

VEGETABLE AND TOFU SKEWERS WITH SEAWEED SATAY : p.81
Sea Spaghetti

STICKY DATE AND WALNUT PUDDING WITH SEA SPAGHETTI : p.83
Sea Spaghetti

LEMON CARDAMOM & SWEET KELP COOKIES: p.87
Sweet Kelp

SWEET KELP CHEESE BALLS : p.89
Sweet Kelp

SEAWEED RELISH : p.94
Mixed Seaweed

OLIVE & ROSEMARY FOCACCIA WITH SEAWEED : p.96
Mixed Seaweed

SEAWEED SALSA : p.98
Mixed Seaweed

MUSHROOM & OLIVE PATE WITH SEA VEG : p.100
Mixed Seaweed

FOREWORD

I grew up in Dungarvan and spent all my summers on the beach, but the only contact with seaweed that I had was when I inadvertently stepped on it while going for a swim... It was a case of doing anything to avoid that slimy green stuff.

The sea plays a big part in my own day to day existence. Every day I look out from the Tannery to see how many boats are out, what the waters like and what fish will I be lucky to get for my menu that evening... The simple truth is I have used seaweed only sporadically over the 15 years at the restaurant. I just don't know enough about it and I don't have time to get it.. Now I know there are very good books out on the subject and I probably need to just apply myself, but despite knowing all the health benefits and the current fashionability of foraging I am not utilising one of the most amazing products that nature has given us....

This fantastic little book is portable, easy, informative, and incredibly well written.
I for one will open my mind to what's around me, get out there with my family and explore this magical slippery green stuff with fresh eyes and renewed enthusiasm... Enjoy

Paul Flynn
The Tannery, Dungarvan
www.tannery.ie
058-45420

Grattan Square, Dungarvan, circa 1904 -
cartloads of seaweed in the foreground.

Image Courtesy of Waterford County Museum
www.waterfordcountyimages.org

This is a guide to the ten most recognisable and abundant edible seaweeds found on the Irish coastline. Each seaweed is described, along with its location on the shore, season for gathering, nutritive value and some recipes to get you started.

Here you are invited to see the rocky shore as a "garden of the sea" and become a sea gardener yourself. Explore a food that was prized by ancient civilisations for its medicinal properties. It is a unique gift from nature and this book will help you to enjoy it. Seaweeds appear as a delicacy in many celebrity chef cookbooks and restaurants, all pointing the way towards using this healthy food in an appetising way. Foraging is fun and sourcing one's food in the wild is deeply satisfying for many people. Whether you are already a forager, want to use novel and nutritional ingredients for your cooking, or want to enrich your family's experience of the shore, there is something in The Sea Gardener for you.

Japan is the country most closely associated with seaweed, where consumption rates are among the highest in the world. In Ireland and Northern Europe, seaweed has been eaten for generations, with carrageen, dilisk and laver bread surviving in folk memory. Sea vegetables, as they are called in Asia, can contain up to ten times more calcium than milk and eight times as much iron as beef. Many scientists attribute Japanese health and longevity to the abundance of seaweed in the diet. This nutrient-dense food is low in calories and high in protein, making it an ideal weight-loss food.

Health food shops and certain supermarkets stock dried Irish seaweed products and these can be used in all of the recipes in this book. If you want to gather your own seaweed, there is the huge satisfaction of going to the seaside and heading home with lunch in a little bag!

the Earth and Ocean seem
To sleep in one another's arms, and dream
Of waves, flowers, clouds, woods, rocks, and all that we
Read in their smiles, and call reality.

from Epipsychidion by Percy Bysshe Shelley (1820)

STAY SAFE ON THE SHORE

- Never forage alone.
- Forage only during calm weather, never when sea is rough, or storms are forecast.
  (Check www.meteireann.ie, www.windguru.com or www.magicseaweed.com).
- Wear non-slip, waterproof footwear. Bring a mobile phone in case of emergency.
- Know the shore. Visit a few times first just to watch the movement of tide.
- Begin foraging an hour before low tide.
- Never turn your back to the sea.
- Squat in a stable position, knees bent, back straight. Hold the plant gently.
- Seaweed for eating should be picked from the rocks, as that lying unattached on the strand may not be clean.

WATER QUALITY

- Only pick seaweeds from clean water. If in any doubt, check water quality in the area with the local authority.
- It's best not to gather near towns, built-up areas or very busy beaches.
- Avoid foraging on beaches with lots of dog-walking and where cars are driven on the beach.

SUSTAINABLE FORAGING

- Collect seaweed during the growing season only, never during the reproductive season. Best times are shown on the Quick find Chart on pages 22-23.
- Take only what you need. It is illegal to harvest seaweed for sale without a licence.
- Seaweeds have 3 parts: the holdfast is root-like and attaches the plant to the rock; the stipe is like a stem and may be very short in some cases; the frond is the "leafy", edible part and that's what you need.
- The size of plants varies hugely, depending on conditions on the shore and not all beaches will have all species mentioned here.
- Cut half or less of the plant, allowing the rest to re-grow. Don't remove the holdfast.
- Use a sharp knife or scissors to cut. Take care with sharp edges on the rocks.
- Rinse the seaweed in clean seawater, removing any small creatures which may be attached.
- Place seaweed in small bags - one for each species will make sorting easier when you get home, but is not essential.
- Collect a little from several rocks, rather than clearing all plants from one area.

- NEVER pull a whole plant from a rock - it will not re-grow.
- About 5-10g of dried seaweed daily is sufficient, so it is not necessary to gather large amounts. If you are new to seaweed, it is recommended that you start with even smaller amounts, allowing your body to adjust gradually to the new food and taste.
- Finally, bring this book with you to help identify the plant in situ. See pages 20-23 for sizes of each type and when and where to find.
- When foraging for land plants, use a good identification book to help you. If in any doubt, consult a botanist as some land plants and fungi are poisonous to humans.

TIDES AND MOONS

- Tides ebb and flow twice daily approximately.
- Tides are highest and lowest on new and full moons, so two days either side of this is best time of fortnight to forage.
- Check tide times in national press, local radio or use tide tables.
- Choose a cool, cloudy day when the seaweed is not heat-stressed or dried out.

DRYING & STORING

All seaweeds can be used fresh from the shore, particularly dilisk, sea lettuce and sea spaghetti. However, in order to benefit from the seaweeds for a longer period, we suggest you take a small bag, a scissors and snip a few pieces to take home, dry and store for future use. At the shore, rinse your cut seaweed in seawater, inspect for wildlife and remove. This is especially important with Carrageen, but all seaweeds provide grazing and shelter for marine snails, topshells and winkles, so expect to find a few of these among the fronds. Seaweed biodegrades rapidly, so keep it cool and proceed with drying as quickly as possible, certainly on the day you gather it.

When you get home, rinse the seaweed in cold water if you want to reduce salt intake. (it is not essential to do this, except with sleabhcan, and is a matter of personal preference). Lay the damp seaweed on a cooling tray, or hang long seaweeds on a drying track, or peg smaller seaweeds onto a clothesline or drying hanger (like a sock-dryer). Let the seaweed drip-dry overnight in a dry place, ideally with a little breeze and out of direct sunlight. Then place in the hot press for another day or so. It may be necessary to turn some seaweeds over to get them dry quickly. By now, the seaweed should be dry but still pliable. It can be stored like this in polythene bags for up to two years.

If you plan to use the seaweed in baking, dry it in a very slow oven (<110 deg C) for 5-10 mins, until crisp. Then rub between fingers to "flake". Now you have a very compact seaweed which will take up little space in the cupboard. Be careful when flaking some of the kelps as they can be sharp when dried like this.

Dried Seaweeds: Sea lettuce, Sleabhcán, Dilisk.

HEALTH BENEFITS

The benefits attributed to seaweed in the diet are wide-ranging and overwhelmingly positive. High in protein, vitamins and minerals, containing little or no fat, seaweed is the perfect food for weight-watchers. Nutrient-dense, it is an excellent addition to a family diet, boosting nutrient levels of meals. High levels of protein, coupled with vitamins B12, C and zinc make it ideal for vegans and vegetarians. Most of the seaweed species used in this book contain B vitamins, vitamins C and E, calcium, iron, magnesium, sodium, copper and potassium, according to research by BIM (Morrissey, J., Kraan, S. & Guiry, M.D. (2001) A Guide to commercially important seaweeds on the Irish coast. Published by Bord lascaigh Mhara, Dun Laoghaire, Co. Dublin). Seaweeds help de-toxify the body and contain high levels of fibre, helping to maintain digestive health. Research into the health benefits of seaweeds is ongoing, and reports are emerging of anti-bacterial, anti-viral, anti-tumour and anti-inflammatory properties.

Carrageen is well-noted as a bronchial cure and a drink made by infusing a tablespoon of it in boiled water and flavouring with lemon and honey will speed recovery from coughs and colds. Nutritionally, the best way to take seaweed is "little and often". A small amount, taken each day, will provide more nourishment and immunity than large amounts taken intermittently. Nutrient levels vary throughout the seasons, for example, bladderwrack has high Vitamin A levels in summer, but in autumn, its vitamin C content is higher. 5-10g dry seaweed is a sufficient daily amount. Start with less, allow your taste buds and gut flora to adjust.

You can also enjoy the emollient and detoxifying effects of seaweed without eating it! Soak in the bath for 30 mins with some serrated wrack to refresh, rejuvenate and re-hydrate your skin. To prepare: Rinse about half a kilo of fresh wrack, and place in bath. Add a litre of boiling water to activate release of the gel, then top up with bathwater. Use the wrack like a loofah or simply soak up the wonder-gel.

Use the wrack on your compost heap afterwards.

Seaweed contains sodium and to reduce salt intake, rinse picked seaweed in fresh water before using. The species listed in this book are, in my experience, the most suitable for eating. However, be careful where you forage for them. Check water quality with the local authority. Seaweeds absorb heavy metals and so should not be consumed from waters which may be contaminated. Avoid areas where you see nutrient-rich streams flowing into the sea - You will know them by the tell-tale profusion of bright green gutweed (*Enteromorpha*) growing on the rocks, and little of any other species. Gutweed is edible and highly nutritious, but because it can be associated with polluted waters, be cautious about consuming it.

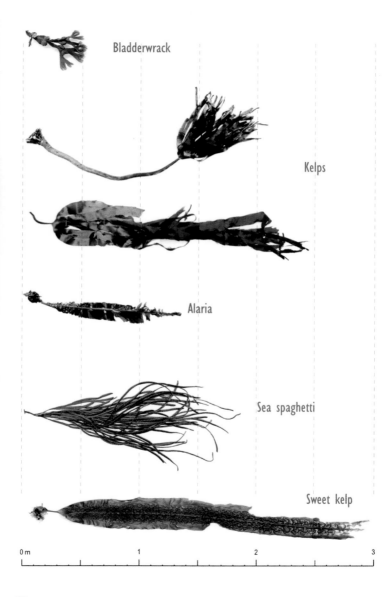

Bladderwrack

Kelps

Alaria

Sea spaghetti

Sweet kelp

0 m   1   2   3

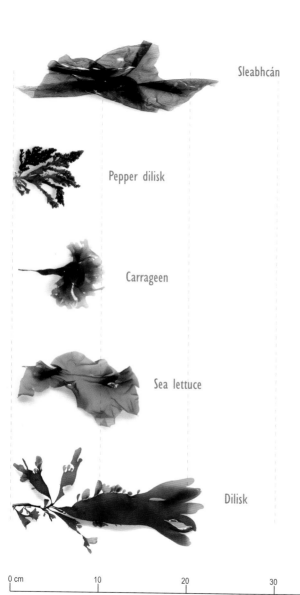

Sleabhcán

Pepper dilisk

Carrageen

Sea lettuce

Dilisk

0 cm   10   20   30   40

SEA

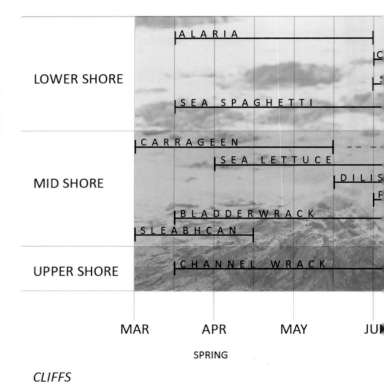

LOWER SHORE | ALARIA | C | | |
SEA SPAGHETTI

MID SHORE | CARRAGEEN | SEA LETTUCE | DILIS | F | BLADDERWRACK | SLEABHCAN

UPPER SHORE | CHANNEL WRACK

|MAR|APR|MAY|JU|

SPRING

CLIFFS

22

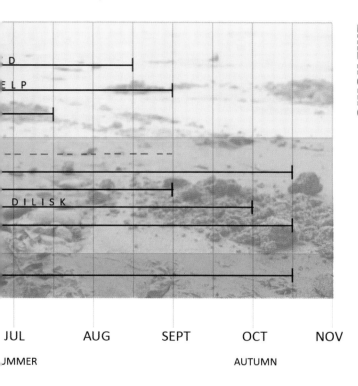

D

E L P

D I L I S K

JUL   AUG   SEPT   OCT   NOV

UMMER   AUTUMN

Jackie Murray from Dunhill gathering Sleabhcán in Annestown in the 70's.

Jackie's sleabhcan was a local speciality, boiled for long hours until soft, placed in jam jars from which it was eaten with a spoon. His son Pat uses the same method and serves the boiled sleabhcan on toast. The family discovered recently that the seaweed gathering tradition had been handed down from Jackie's mother.

TOP
TEN
EDIBLE
SEAWEEDS

CARRAGEEN

Chondrus crispus
CARAGÍN   CARRAGEEN MOSS

MID SHORE
MARCH - MAY
RED - PURPLE

DESCRIPTION
- Purplish-red in colour, blanches in strong sunlight.
- Up to 15cm in length.
- Grows in "bushy" clusters. Almost floral appearance. Frond is divided evenly to show a multi-branched fan-like structure.
- Blades of fronds are flat and stencil-like at the tip.
- Grows on rocks or stones in mid to lower shore. When in water, fronds may appear iridescent.

FORAGING
Best gathered during summer. Similar to grape pip weed (*Mastocarpus stellatus*) which may grow alongside it, however, the tips, unlike carrageen, are rough. Cut carrageen well above the holdfast. It is advised not to gather too much in one area but to move here and there along the shore in order to allow the plant to re-seed and grow. Do not gather in late autumn and winter when plant is fertile.

CARRAGEEN CHOCOLATE AND LIME PUDDING

15g dried carrageen
600 mls milk
125g dark chocolate
grated zest and juice of 2 limes
3 tblspns caster sugar or honey
1 egg, yolk and white separated

Soak the carrageen in cold water for 10 mins approx.

Transfer the carrageen to a saucepan and add milk and lime zest. Bring to the boil and simmer gently until thick enough to coat the back of a spoon. Make sure it does not boil.

Strain through a fine sieve and break the chocolate into the warm milk mixture.

Add half the lime juice and allow to cool a little.

Mix the egg yolk with 2 tblspns of the sugar in a bowl and add the chocolate liquid.

Whisk the egg white stiffly and fold into the mixture.

Place in serving glasses and refrigerate until set, about 20-30 mins.

Make a syrup by gently heating half the lime juice and a tablespoon of sugar. Allow to cool.

Serve the pudding cold with mascarpone or whipped cream and some lime syrup spooned over the top.

SALMON MOUSSE

250g salmon or sea trout
½ stock cube
3 tblspns lemon juice
120 mls mayonnaise
120 mls double cream
2 tblspns tomato puree
1 tblspn chopped fresh dill (or half tblspn dried)
25g carrageen
Salt and pepper

Poach fish in about 200 mls of stock for a few mins. Remove fish and reserve stock.

Put carrageen into reserved stock, bring to the boil and simmer until it thickens.

Flake fish, remove skin and any bones. Allow to cool.

Blend lemon juice, mayonnaise, tomato puree, dill and mix with fish.

Add stock to fish mix and stir in well. Refrigerate until almost set.

Whip cream and fold into fish mixture,

Pour into mould and leave in fridge until set. Turn out on plate and garnish.

DILISK

Palmaria palmata

DUILEASC   DULSE

MID SHORE

MID MAY – SEPTEMBER

RED – BROWN

DESCRIPTION

- Red seaweed, 10-30 cm long, frond is soft, smooth and branched, like fingers on a hand.
- Found mid-shore to lower shore.
- Grows on top of rocks exposed at low tide, or hangs from sheltered side of rocks.
- Also grows on other seaweeds, particularly kelp stipes.

FORAGING

Best gathered in spring and summer. Cut one or two "fingers" from each plant, leaving the remainder to re-grow. Do not gather in winter when plant is fertile.

CULINARY USES

Dilisk is a tasty seaweed and can be eaten fresh from the rocks, or chopped finely and added to salads, mashed potatoes and omelettes. To store for longer term use, it can be dried by wrapping in brown paper and leaving in a hot press. This results in a soft, chewy texture, ideal for snacking on.

Dried dilisk should be reconstituted in water for 10 mins before use.

GARDEN AND SEA RISOTTO

Seasonal Vegetables (asparagus, chard, peas, green beans, mangetout, mushrooms, radicchio, spinach, watercress, root vegetables, onions) - about 2 handfuls

25g dried dilisk, soaked in water for 5 minutes

320g arborio rice

1 litre warm stock

150 mls white wine

50g parmesan/hard cheese

3 cloves garlic

50g butter

50 mls oil

Steam summer vegetables lightly / roast root vegetables, depending on which you're using. Melt butter and oil in a large saucepan.

Stew onions and garlic for a few minutes.

Add rice and fry gently for a few minutes, ensuring it doesn't burn.

Add ladle of stock. Stir continually, adding stock as it absorbs.

Add wine and parmesan.

Stir in previously cooked vegetables and dilisk. You can add herbs to suit if you wish, or sprinkle on top before serving.

Mushrooms can be mixed in OR if using fresh / wild mushrooms, fry separately in butter and serve over risotto.

Shown here with wild irish mushrooms and fried gutweed (*Enteromorpha*).

BEETROOT AND DILISK BREAD

This can be eaten as a tea bread or with soup or salad

20g dried dilisk - soaked in water
110g butter - melted
175g fresh beetroot - peeled and grated
3 large free range eggs
20g caster sugar (optional)
250g plain white or spelt flour
1½ tsps baking powder

Drain and chop dilisk.
Brush loaf tin with butter.
Combine remaining butter, beetroot, eggs, sugar and dilisk.
Fold in sieved flour and baking powder.
Turn mixture into loaf tin and bake for 40-50 mins. at 180 deg C.
Cool before turning out.
This bread is moist, so can be eaten without butter.

SLEABHCÁN

Porphyra spp.

SLEABHAC · LAVER · PURPLE LAVER · NORI

MID SHORE
MARCH - MID APRIL
DARK RED - BLACK

DESCRIPTION

- Dark red seaweed, though may appear dark green or black.
- Up to 20-30 cm long, very thin frond, almost transparent.
- Turns almost black when dried.
- Found on upper to mid-shore though some species grow on lower shore.
- Grows on rocks exposed at low tide, resembles melted black plastic draped over low rocks.
- (Pronounced "slou-caun").

FORAGING

Best harvested after the first frost — December/January until April. Collect after calm weather if possible, as stormy seas leave unbelievable amounts of sand among the delicate fronds. Do not gather in early winter when plant is fertile.

CULINARY USES

Rinse thoroughly several times with tap water, until all sand is removed. Sleabhcán can be dried or used fresh. Dry by laying on cooling tray for 24 hours. Or boil fresh for laver bread. It requires long periods of boiling to soften — up to 4 hours. Freezing the rinsed, fresh seaweed first may help shorten cooking time. It can be used in savoury and sweet dishes, even with chocolate!

Nori sheets used in sushi are closely related to sleabhcán and are made using mechanical drying and spraying.

41

CARROT AND SLEABHCÁN CAKE

200g carrots, grated
2 tblspns sleabhcán, dried, flaked and reconstituted in a little water
175g dark brown sugar
2 large free range eggs
150 mls sunflower oil
100g wholemeal flour and 100g white flour
1 tsp baking powder
2 tsps mixed spice
1 tsp bread soda
grated zest of an orange
130g sultanas
50g dessicated coconut
50g walnuts toasted lightly

[For the Syrup]:
juice of an orange
1 tblspn lemon juice
75g soft dark brown sugar.
Blend these 3 together in a cup using a small whisk/fork.

Whisk sugar, eggs and oil together until sugar is dissolved (2-3 mins).
Fold sifted dry ingredients into this mixture.
Finally, fold in orange and remaining ingredients, along with sleabhcán.
Bake in a lined and oiled 20 cm round cake tin for approx. 40 mins at 170 deg C. When dry in centre, remove from oven and pour syrup over.
Allow to cool for 10 mins in tin.
This cake can be decorated using cream cheese/mascarpone cheese mixed with honey, and then sprinkling chopped nuts / grated orange rind on top.

✱ v nice!

LAVER BREAD

This is a traditional Welsh dish and here is a vegetarian version which works well as a snack, or as a breakfast accompaniment, just like the classic version. It is shown here as a starter, served with apple sauce.

120g cooked sleabhcán, drained and chopped finely
(To cook sleabhcán, place in large saucepan after rinsing, and cover generously with cold water. Bring to the boil and boil for 2-3 hours until soft. "Poke" seaweed under water at regular intervals)
50g oatmeal flour or ground oatflakes
Butter or oil for frying
1 onion, finely chopped
salt and pepper
pinch grated nutmeg

Mix the sleabhcán, oatmeal and nutmeg.
Soft-fry the onion in butter.
Mix thoroughly with the sleabhcán mixture, until it all "comes together".
Make small cakes using damp hands, 1-2 cm thick.
Heat butter/oil in frying pan and fry the cakes for 1-2 minutes each side.
Drain on kitchen paper and serve with scrambled free range eggs for a delicious breakfast.

PEPPER DILISK

Osmundea pinnatifida   PEPPER DULSE

MÍOBHÁN

MID SHORE

JUNE - OCTOBER

RED - BROWN

DESCRIPTION

- Red / Dark Purple Seaweed with brown stipe and flattened fronds.
- About 10cm in length, although sometimes longer in late summer.
- Grows in small thick clumps and is held on rocks with strong holdfasts.
- Found on mid - lower shore.
- Very pungent smell.
- Colour darkens when dried.
- Consume in moderation, due to high content of terapenes.

FORAGING

Pepper dilisk usually grows on top of rocks as it can withstand long periods out of water. It is best gathered in early spring. The short stipe does make it difficult to grip the young plant. Cut one or two of the fronds at the base before moving to a different clump. Do not gather in late spring when the plant is fertile.

CULINARY USES

Tiny amounts are used in cookery as this is a strong-tasting seaweed. Sprinkle a half teaspoon of dried pepper dilisk on a baked savoury dish to give a peppery flavour.

CARAMELISED RED ONION TARTLETS WITH GOATS CHEESE AND PEPPER DILISK

Pastry

170g plain flour
70g butter
50g cheddar cheese, grated finely
3 tblspns cold water
1 egg, beaten

Sift flour. Cut butter into small pieces and rub into flour until the mixture resembles breadcrumbs. Add some water and blend using a knife. Add more water if necessary to make a smooth dough. Place in a polythene bag and chill for 20 mins. Roll pastry out thinly and line oiled, fluted, loose-bottomed tart tins (12cm diameter, 3cm high). Bake at 180 deg C for 15 mins. Cool on a wire tray in the tins.

Filling

3 red onions
(approx. 400g)
4 tblspns balsamic vinegar
1 tblspn chopped fresh sage
1 tsp chopped dried pepper dilisk
some small sprigs to decorate
25g butter
splash of red wine (optional)
100g mild goats cheese, sliced into 4 rounds

Melt butter and add onions, balsamic vinegar, sage, pepper dilisk and wine if using. Cook over a low heat for about 30 mins until onions are soft and liquid is absorbed. Allow to cool. Brush pastry cases within beaten egg and cook for just 5 mins, to seal the pastry. Divide the onion mixture between the pastry cases, place the goats cheese on top, add a sprig of pepper dilisk on top and bake for 15 mins. Remove from tins and serve hot.

RICE & VEGETABLE FRITTATA WITH PEPPER DILISK

This is a great way to use up leftover cooked rice. It's an ideal student recipe too — quick, nutritious and tasty.

Frittata

200g cooked brown rice
1 large carrot, grated
1 courgette, grated
Small tin of corn kernels
1 onion, sliced
5 eggs
2 tblspns rapeseed or other vegetable oil
1 tsp pepper dilisk
2 tblspns chopped basil
100g grated cheese (Gruyere used here)

Coconut Cream Sauce

100g yogurt
100 g coconut cream
1 tblspn chopped fresh mint or coriander

Heat half of the oil in frying pan and gently sweat the onion.
Add carrots and courgette and cook for about 5 mins.
Mix together the rice, vegetables, pepper dilisk and basil in a bowl.
Beat eggs a little with a fork and add to the mixture with the corn.
Heat remainder of oil in frying pan and turn the mixture onto the pan.
Cook over a very low heat for about 10 mins., ensuring it does not stick to the pan.
Grate cheese on top and finish under grill for about 5 mins. until cheese is melted.
To make the cream, simply mix the yogurt, coconut cream and herb in a container and shake well.
Cut into 4 pieces and serve with coconut cream and salad on the side.

who owns the seaweed ?

Pats Burns, who lived at Whitfield, between Fenor and Annestown, was a great storyteller and native Irish speaker, and was recorded in the '60s by the local priest and the doctor. He told the story of his mothers' and neighbours' imprisonment at the hands of the Pallisers of Annestown (the local landlord) for trespassing on "their" beach. Washed-up seaweed was commonly used to fertilise potato plots. These women spent 4 weeks in gaol in Tramore, for gathering it on Annestown Strand, around 1900. They refused the offer of the parish priest to pay the fine to Palliser and allow their release, aggrieved that the landlord should profit from what nature had provided free.

Story taken from recording of Pats Burns
Courtesy Stella Whittle RIP.

SEA LETTUCE

Ulva lactuca   Ulva spp.

GLASÁN

MID SHORE

APRIL - OCTOBER

GREEN

DESCRIPTION

- Bright green seaweed with wide, wavy fronds, very like land lettuce.
- Attached by small holdfast.
- Grows mainly in mid to lower shore area, often near dilisk, and in rock pools.
- Grows rapidly in summer.
- Similar in colour to *Enteromorpha* (gutweed), but sea lettuce fronds are much wider.

FORAGING

Gather through summer, plants do get tougher when older. Avoid collecting near sewage or run-off from agricultural land as it may be contaminated. Do not gather in late winter/early spring when plant is fertile.

CULINARY USES

Sea lettuce is a delicate seaweed which works well in salads when fresh. Soak in cold water with a squeeze of lemon juice for 20 mins before using fresh. When dried and mixed with dilisk, it makes a colourful and tasty condiment.

SEA LETTUCE WRAP WITH HUMMUS

12 sea lettuce "leaves" (depends on size)
20 cm strip of kelp
200g chickpeas, soaked overnight
2 cloves garlic, crushed
2 tblspns tahini
1 tsp dried mixed seaweed, soaked in water for 10 mins
1 tblspn chopped fresh coriander
½ tsp mustard
3 tblspns olive oil
juice of 1 lemon

Boil chickpeas with strip of kelp until soft - about 1 hour.
Cool and transfer to blender.
Add all ingredients except oil and blend until well mixed.
Add oil gradually until texture is smooth but firm.
Soak sea lettuce in hot water for 10 mins.
Lay out flat (overlapping fronds if small) to make 12 roughly rectangular shapes.
Place 2 tblspns hummus filling in centre of palm and form into a cylinder shape.
Place on sea lettuce.
Roll seaweed so that you have a green wrap around the hummus filling.
Serve as a snack or starter with sushi ginger and soy on the side.

FORAGER'S SALAD

This is a seasonal salad, best made in spring with fresh greens. Collect wild greens from pollution-free areas, away from roadsides where car exhaust will poison them.

Be sure about which plants to pick and rinse before using.

small bunch each of dandelion leaves, chickweed, borage, lesser celandine, silverweed and watercress leaves

some marigold flower heads or nasturtiums

one or two wild garlic leaves

a few hawthorn leaves

or use your favourite wild leaves (mix will vary with season)

2-3 fronds of sea lettuce, snipped into small pieces. Dried sea lettuce can be re-constituted in water in 5 mins.

2-3 dilisk fronds, snipped into very small pieces

half head of garden lettuce

some lightly toasted pine nuts

2 tblspns olive oil

1 tblspn cider vinegar

1 tsp wholegrain mustard

1 tblspn local honey

Rinse leaves and dry. Place in serving bowl.

Add sea lettuce and dilisk.

Mix oil, mustard, honey and then add vinegar.

Dress and toss salad. Sprinkle pine nuts on top and serve.

In autumn, you could sprinkle some chopped toasted hazelnuts on top and drop in a blackberry or two.

ALARIA
Alaria esculenta
LÁIR   WAKAME
SEA FERN   DABBERLOCKS   FERN WEED

LOWER SHORE
MID MARCH - JUNE
BROWN - DARK GREEN

ALARIA

DESCRIPTION

- Brown seaweed with golden-brown fronds usually about 1m long and about 6 cm wide but can grow to twice that size.
- Short frills at the base, more delicate fronds and a mid-rib distinguish alaria from other kelps.
- Closely related to Japanese Wakame and is traditionally added to miso soup.

FORAGING

Gather in spring and mid summer when plant is at its best. Not always easy to find, alaria grows on the lower shore and often on exposed rocky shores. Cut frond at leat half way up from base. Do not gather in winter when plant is fertile.

ALARIA AND BRAISED VEGETABLES WITH NOODLES

25g dried chopped alaria (stalk removed), soaked in 200 mls water for 10 mins.

2 tblspns sunflower oil

1 kg prepared vegetables of your choice — carrot, scallion, onion, broccoli, mangetout, red pepper, pak choi and mushroom

1 tblspn grated root ginger

2 garlic cloves, peeled, crushed and chopped

200 mls warm miso boullion stock made with alaria soak-water

1 tblspn cornflour

3 tblspns tamari or soy sauce

250g medium noodles

200g firm tofu

Black pepper

2 tblspns chopped coriander

1 tblspn sesame oil *	1 garlic clove, minced *
2 tblspns sunflower oil *	2 tblpsns sesame seeds, toasted *
1 tblspn crunchy peanut butter *	3 tblpsns tamari or soy sauce *
½ chilli, chopped finely *	juice of ½ lime *

Prepare the noodle dressing by blending all of the ingredients marked * until smooth. Heat the oil in a large wok and add the vegetables. Stir-fry for 2-3 mins. Add the miso stock and alaria. Cover and cook for another 2 mins. Blend the cornflour with soy sauce. Remove the braised vegetables and place in a warm bowl. Add the cornflour/soy sauce to the wok and cook stirring continuously, for a few minutes, until the sauce thickens. Season with pepper. Return the vegetables to the wok, stir gently into sauce to warm through. Cook the noodles according to instructions on packet. Stir in the prepared dressing. Serve hot with the braised vegetables and some coriander sprinkled on top.

OATY APPLE BOWL WITH ALARIA

*This is a hearty, dairy-free, warming breakfast — alaria gives a
mild nutty flavour which works well with the apple.*

200g flaked oatmeal
150 mls apple juice
150 mls water
20g dried alaria
30g sultanas (or dried fruit)
1 tblspn lightly toasted almonds or hazelnut

Soak dried fruit and flaked alaria overnight in water.
Add to oatmeal and apple juice in a saucepan or double-boiler.
Cook gently for 3 mins until most liquid has been absorbed and porridge is
creamy.
Take care not to overcook.
Mix in nuts and serve with apple and honey to taste.

BLADDERWRACK

Fucus vesiculosus

CARRCHONLA   FEAMAINN BHOILGÍNEACH

MID SHORE
MID MARCH - MID OCTOBER
BROWN - DARK GREEN

DESCRIPTION

When people think of seaweed, they are quite likely to first think of the brown, slippery, or "knobbly" seaweeds that grow on the coast, and also in estuaries, clinging to quay walls anywhere the water is even a little salty. These are the wracks, an adaptable and robust species. Some wracks are tasty, others more suitable as animal feed or use as a beauty therapy.

- Bladderwrack is a brown seaweed, found mainly on the mid-shore.
- Usually grows to about 40 cm, although size varies considerably depending on conditions.
- It can appear olive green or deep brown, but is identifiable by its air bladders, found in pairs along the frond, at either side of mid-rib.
- Note the difference between the rounded air bladders on this plant, unlike the egg-shaped ones on eggwrack, or the spiral fronds on spiral wrack. Channelwrack does not have air bladders.

FORAGING

Best gathered in mid-late summer. Remove only selected branches from several different plants. Cut above the short stipe.

CULINARY USES

Use dried and crumbled with mixed seaweeds in savoury dishes.
It is successfully teamed with ginger in the gingercake recipe on page 73.

TOMATO AND BLADDERWRACK SAUCE

2 x 400g tins of plum tomatoes
1 red onion
1 tblspn dried crumbled bladderwrack, reconstituted in water for 10 mins.
1 clove of garlic
1 tblspn olive oil
½ small red chilli, chopped finely
1 tsp dried oregano
1 tsp red wine vinegar
1 tsp brown sugar
a few leaves of fresh basil or marjoram, chopped roughly
ground black pepper

Gently sweat onion and garlic in olive oil.
Add chilli, tomatoes, bladderwrack and oregano and continue to simmer gently for 30 mins.
Add vinegar, sugar and fresh basil and season to taste.
Serve with pasta. Reduce by half to use as pizza topping.
This sauce can be refrigerated for up to a week or frozen for up to a month.
Eat with your favourite pasta with some toasted almonds sprinkled on top.

ORANGE GINGERCAKE WITH BLADDERWRACK

50g dried bladderwrack, ground
225g wholemeal flour
1½ tsps ground ginger
1½ tsps baking powder
½ tsp bread soda
225g brown sugar
2 tblspns treacle / molasses
75g butter
4 tblspns milk
1 free range egg
grated rind of 1 small orange
2 tblspns orange juice

Put first five ingredients in a mixing bowl.
Heat together sugar, treacle and butter until butter is melted.
Combine all ingredients together, beat well and pour into greased 27 x 18 cm shallow cake tin.
Bake at 170 deg C for about 30 mins., until firm to touch.
Cool in tin, dust with icing sugar, then cut into squares.

Gingercake is prone to sinking a little in the centre if oven door is opened too soon, or if it is baked in too deep a tin.

KELP / OARWEED
Laminaria digitata

CHOPÓG   KOMBU   KELP   TANGLEWEED

LOWER SHORE
JUNE - AUGUST
BROWN

DESCRIPTION

- Brown colour. Long flat leather-like ribbons.
- Oarweed can be up to 2m long and 60cm wide.
- Strong holdfast and long, rough, inflexible stipe. The frond is usually split into a large finger-like blade.
- Found on the lower shore securely attached to the rocks.

FORAGING

Gather at low spring tides from early spring to late summer. Cut frond at least half-way up from base. A similar species (called forest kelp, also edible) but with smooth, flexible stipe can be gathered only in high summer and mid-winter.

CULINARY USES

Include a 15cm strip when cooking dried beans to speed up cooking, add nutrients and improve digestibility. If using dried kelp, reconstitute in water for 5 to 10 mins. If you want ground kelp, put it into a cool oven for a few minutes. It's ready when it crumbles easily - use a pestle and mortar to grind. Add a strip of kelp to soup when adding stock and remove before blending / serving. This is a good way to introduce kelp to your diet. Or if you prefer, leave the kelp in the soup - chopped into small pieces first. All the kelps contain alginates which are used commercially as food additives - thickeners, stabilisers and gelling agents (E402-E405).

THAI BEAN AND KELP CURRY

200g of mixed dried beans (e.g. pinto, haricot, cannelloni, mung, aduki, soya, chick peas)

strip of dried kelp about 20cms, soaked in cold water for 5 mins and cut into small pieces

1 large onion, sliced

2 cloves of garlic crushed

1 tsp peanut or vegetable oil

1 tblspn fresh chopped coriander

1 tsp cumin

1 tsp turmeric

small red chilli, finely chopped

1 tblspn grated root ginger

2 carrots chopped

1 tblspn red curry paste

125g of any of the following chopped - aubergine, cauliflower, red pepper, courgette, french beans

300 mls light coconut milk

1 tblspn peanut butter

2 tsps lime rind, finely grated

2 tblspns chopped fresh basil

Soak the beans in cold water over night.

Cook the beans with kelp for about an hour or until just tender. Drain.

Saute onion, garlic, coriander, turmeric and cumin in a little oil for 3 mins.

Add carrot and cook for another 5 mins.

Add rest of ingredients and simmer for 15 mins.

Season to taste.

Serve with rice, noodles or naan bread.

SPICED BUTTERNUT SQUASH & APPLE SOUP WITH KELP

500g peeled or deseeded butternut squash, chopped into 2cm cubes
1 onion, peeled & chopped
1 cooking apple
20cm strip of kelp
1.5 litre stock
15g butter or 1tbspln oil
1 clove garlic, crushed & chopped
2 bay leaves
1 cinnamon stick

Gently fry onion, garlic, bay leaf & spices in melted butter or oil for 5 mins.
Add the squash & apple & cook covered for about 10 mins.
Add stock & pepper.
Snip kelp into 0.5cm pieces & add to soup.
Bring to the boil., reduce heat & simmer for 35-40 mins.
Remove bay leaf & cinnamon.
Blend the soup until smooth.
Adjust seasoning & serve hot.

SEA SPAGHETTI

Himanthalia elongata THONGWEED

RìSEACH

LOWER SHORE
MID MARCH - JULY
BROWN - DARK GREEN

DESCRIPTION

- Brown seaweed, strands grow up to 2m in length with a diameter of 5 - 8 mm.
- Grows from a small button-like base in early spring. Found at very low tide levels. As the name suggests, this looks like brown spaghetti.

FORAGING

Best gathered when young and tender. The fronds become flat and "warty" when older. Cut one or two strands from each plant. Check for blue-rayed limpets (2-3 mm long with distinctive blue stripes on back) which attach in large numbers, especially in late summer. Pick these off and place on another seaweed before cutting.

CULINARY USES

Use this seaweed fresh from the sea. Soak in water for 5-10 mins and chop into salads or add to cooked vegetables for a savoury flavour and slightly crunchy texture.

VEGETABLE AND TOFU SKEWERS WITH SEAWEED SATAY

1 (225g) tin braised tofu*
2 red peppers chopped into 1 cm pieces
2 courgettes, sliced thickly
1 red onion, cut into segments
8 button mushrooms
8 wooden skewers soaked in water for 20 mins

Satay Sauce

20g sea spaghetti, chopped finely and soaked in 200 mls water for 10 mins.
200g crunchy peanut butter
2 cloves garlic, minced
½ red chilli, chopped finely
1 tblspn tamari / soy sauce
1 tblspn lemon juice
1 tsp brown sugar

Marinade

100 mls tamari / soy sauce
50 mls dry sherry
2 tblspns honey

Combine marinade ingredients and place in a shallow dish.
Thread the prepared vegetables and cubed tofu onto skewers and place in the marinade, covered, for 30 mins, turning once. Cook under a hot grill for about 10 mins, brushing frequently with marinade. Turn to grill evenly on all sides.

Place all satay sauce ingredients in a small saucepan, including the soak water. Cook gently for about 10 mins., adding more water if necessary. Pour sauce over grilled vegetables and tofu and serve hot.

*Braised tofu is a soybean curd which is marinated in miso giving it a delicious savoury taste and brown colour. It is available tinned and ready-to-eat in health food shops.

STICKY DATE AND WALNUT PUDDING WITH SEA SPAGHETTI

125g butter
125g soft brown sugar
200 mls cream
125g self-raising flour
125g chopped dates
50g chopped walnuts
25g dried sea spaghetti, soaked in 100 mls water for 30 mins and finely chopped.
1 egg
½ tsp bread soda

Preheat the oven to 180 deg C.
Place dates in bowl and sprinkle the bread soda over.
Remove sea spaghetti from water.
Warm the water and pour over the dates.
Allow to stand for 10 mins.
Make the sauce by placing 75g butter, 75g sugar and the cream in a saucepan.
Heat gently until butter is melted, then boil rapidly for about 3 mins until caramel colour develops.
Cover the base of a greased 1litre oven-proof dish with a little of the sauce.
Cream the remaining butter and sugar together.
Beat in the egg and sea spaghetti.
Add the date mixture and finally, fold in the flour and walnuts.
Pour into the oven dish and bake for about 45 mins.
Cool slightly and turn out onto a plate.
Heat the sauce and pour over the pudding and serve warm.
Delicious!

SWEET KELP

Saccharina latissima

RUFA SWEET KOMBU SEA BELT SUGAR KELP

LOWER SHORE
APRIL - OCTOBER
BROWN - DARK GREEN

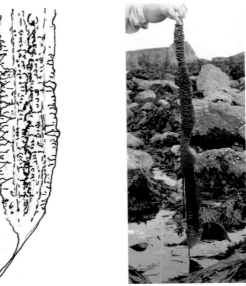

DESCRIPTION

- Brown seaweed. Can look brown-yellow with strong holdfast and short stipe.
- Single long frond is ruffled and feels rough to touch. Some say it resembles the back of a crocodile. Distinctive and easy to recognise.
- Common on the lower shore and intertidal pools.

FORAGING

Spring to autumn is the best time to gather. Cut the top section of the frond, leaving at least 10cm of blade above the stipe. Do not gather in winter when plant is fertile.

CULINARY USES

Sweet Kelp contains mannitol, a natural sugar, and so works best when dried, ground/flaked and added to sweet things such as cakes and cookies. The sugar may dry to a white powder on the frond - this is quite normal.

LEMON CARDAMOM COOKIES WITH SWEET KELP

125g softened butter
125g light brown sugar
1 large egg
350g plain flour
1½ tsps grated lemon rind
½ tsp ground cardamom seeds
½ tsp sweet kelp dried and ground

Cream the butter, then add sugar and cream again until light and fluffy.
Beat in the egg.
Fold in the sifted, dry ingredients.
Knead briefly.
Chill the dough for 30 mins.
Pick about a large tablespoon of dough and roll into a ball, place on lightly
oiled baking tray and flatten slightly.
Bake at 180 dec C for 10 - 12 mins or until lightly browned.
Place on cooling tray.
This makes about 12 cookies. They will store in an airtight container for a
few days.

SWEET KELP CHEESE BALLS

These make an ideal party snack - tasty and a talking point!

long strip of sweet kelp, cut into twelve 3 cm pieces
150g cream cheese
150g Cashel Blue cheese
50g cheddar cheese, grated
bunch fresh parsley, finely chopped
50g walnuts, toasted and finely chopped

Mix parsley and walnut together and place on plate.
Mash blue cheese with cream cheese.
Add grated cheddar and mix well.
Season with cracked black pepper.
Using 2 small spoons, make a ball of cheese mix, and
roll in walnut/parsley mix.
Place on clean plate. Refrigerate for 20 mins.
Crisp the sweet kelp pieces in 120 deg C oven for 5-10 mins.
Watch closely so that kelp doesn't burn.
Allow to cool, 5 mins approx. The kelp pieces will be light and crisp.
Place one cheese ball on each sweet kelp piece when ready to eat.
These snacks are best assembled when ready to use, as the kelp toughens
after an hour or two.

The town of Tramore, Co. Waterford has a long tradition of marking the end of the summer by parading a life-sized doll, draped in seaweed, around the town and throwing her into the sea on the feast of St. Michael, the patron saint of seafarers. In the early 1900s, the women who worked on the beach managing the bathing huts and assisting visiting bathers, were an important part of the town's culture. At the close of the season, they carried the seaweed doll (known as Michil or Breedeen) through the town, collecting gratuities from townspeople as they went.

Now an annual surf and sea festival has revived the ritual, using a 21st century wicker doll, made by local crafts woman, Cathy Hayden.

MIXED SEAWEEDS

SEAWEED RELISH

This condiment can be used as a topping on savoury dishes, as a sandwich flavouring or simply spread on rice crackers or toast.

50g dried bladderwrack
50g dried kelp
100g fresh sleabhchan / 25g dried
2 tblspns fresh white breadcrumbs
150g butter
¼ tsp cayenne
½ tsp mixed spice
½ tsp dried oregano
Ground black pepper

Reconstitute dried seaweed with hot water for 30 mins.
Place in saucepan with soak liquor, add fresh seaweed and bring to boil.
Boil until sleabhcan becomes mushy.
Drain and transfer to food processor.
Blend to a paste using cooking water if necessary.
Stir in breadcrumbs, spices, pepper.
Place in ceramic bowl, cover, chill and serve with eggs or add to savoury sauces.
Store in the fridge and use within a week, or store in sterilised jar in fridge for up to a week.

OLIVE & ROSEMARY FOCACCIA WITH SEAWEED

Making yeast bread is one of the most satisfying cooking experiences. Give yourself some time, a warm kitchen and follow this recipe to make 4 smallish focaccia breads. They are perfect with soup or salad.

350g plain flour
350g strong flour
1 tblspn salt
2 x 7g sachets yeast
2 tblspns sugar
1 tblspn mixed seaweed
600 mls tepid water

Dissolve the yeast and sugar in about half of the tepid water.

Place the flours, salt and seaweed in a large bowl. Make a well in the centre. Pour the dissolved yeast mixture into the well, add the rest of the warm water and stir by hand to draw in all of the flour. Knead the dough for a good 5 minutes on a flat, floured surface. Place the dough on an oiled baking tray, score once or twice with a knife cover with a large polythene bag or clingfilm and leave to "prove" in a warm place (a cool oven or hotpress if the kitchen isn't already warm). This could take up to an hour, until the dough has doubled in size.

Take the raised dough onto the floured surface again, and knead some more, for about a minute. (This is called "knocking back"). Cut the dough into 4 equal pieces and place on floured baking trays, flattening it out to make a roughly circular shape about 2 cm thick. Leave to prove a second time, until it doubles in size again. Then "poke" the bread here and there to make little holes and pop in some olives. Dip the rosemary leaves in olive oil and scatter these on top. Bake in the over at 230 deg C. for about 15 mins. Brush with olive oil and use as soon as cool enough. It stores for a few days too. The topping can be varied to suit your tastes, or left plain.

SEAWEED SALSA

This recipe was first sampled on Kilfarassey beach, Co. Waterford on a cold spring day in 2007. It passed the taste test! A spoonful or two works well with the salmon mousse and on the focaccia bread.

half a cucumber
9 cherry tomatoes
2 scallions
1 tblspn mixed seaweed, reconstituted in a little water
1 tblspn chopped dill
dressing: use recipe on page 59

Chop vegetables into even-sized pieces.
Add dill, seaweed and dressing.
Mix gently but thoroughly.
Ideally chill before eating.

MUSHROOM and OLIVE PATE WITH SEA VEG

1 onion

3 cloves garlic

175g mushrooms

75g black olives, stoned

175g ripe vine tomatoes, peeled

1 tblspn oil

1 tblspn mixed seaweed

1 tbspn tomato puree

2 tsps fresh thyme (or 1 tsp dried)

1 tsp dried oregano

½ tsp miso bouillon powder or 1/2 stock cube

1 tsp sugar

150 mls red wine / water

Chop all vegetables as finely as possible.

Heat the oil and sweat the inion and garlic for a few minutes.

Add the mushrooms and cook for another few minutes.

Then add the tomatoes, olives, seaweed, herbs, bouillon and sugar and stir well.

Cook for 5 mins, then add the wine and simmer for 15-20 mins. Season.

Serve cold as a snack, with perhaps with some strips of raw carrot, celery, cucumber and fresh bread, or simply as a snack on toast.

"We need the tonic of wildness...At the same time that we are earnest to explore and learn all things, we require that all things be mysterious and unexplorable, that land and sea be indefinitely wild, unsurveyed and unfathomed by us because unfathomable. We can never have enough of nature."

Henry David Thoreau, Walden: or, Life in the Woods, (1854)

When we go to the rocky shore to forage for seaweed, we find ourselves in a rich mosaic of wildlife. The rocks and pools are filled with life; Barnacles, mussels, lichens, limpets, crabs, fish, dog whelks, starfish, topshells, anenomes, sea hares, urchins, winkles, shrimps and so on, co-exist with the seaweed in a habitat defined by the rocks, the aspect, the location, as well as the ocean and tides. In this unique environment, all life grows, multiplies, reproduces, dies and decomposes in a cycle which is in tune with the passing seasons. It does this best when there is no intrusion from humans. We are stepping into a world which existed long before people arrived on this island nine thousand, or so years ago. Every step we take on the rocks is significant: we are like giant Gullivers among the littoral Lilliputians and our approach must be gentle and respectful if we want to co-exist with these other species. Here we take a closer look at what is going on around us on the rocky shore.

The colour of the seaweeds is probably what we first notice: the browns of the wracks and kelps, the purplish red of carrageen and dilisk and the striking bright green of sea lettuce. All seaweeds, like green land plants, photosynthesise when immersed - that is, they make food from sunlight, using nutrients absorbed from seawater. And because water absorbs light, reducing what's available to a submerged plant, the light-absorbing red and brown ("accessory") pigments in seaweed allows them to grow even in the depths. They multiply by producing spores which are carried by seawater, attach to a rock and grow into a new plant. In winter and early spring, new plants can be seen emerging, just as in a garden. Seaweeds are classed biologically as marine algae and have been on earth as long as one million years ago, according to the fossil record.

We notice that some seaweeds are partly immersed in water or grow in rock pools, such as the sea lettuce and the large forest kelp. Others, like sleabhcán, are draped over rocks and may even dry out between tides. Barnacles are out of water at low tide, and covered six hours later when the tide comes in. There is a pattern to this, whichever shore we're on — plants and animals seem to have preferred locations or bands in which they occur. Ecologists call this pattern "zonation". The zones are usually referred to as: Splash; Intertidal — made up of upper, middle and lower shore - and Subtidal zones. (Scientists also use the term Littoral zones and fringes). Plant and animal species which can tolerate dessication will be found on the upper shore, which is out of water for the longest period of time each day; those that cannot recover from drying out will be closer to the lower shore. The bands or zones can be quite narrow and obvious, especially on steep shores, less so on gradually sloping shores. The zones are largely defined by the environmental gradient between land and sea, the twice daily rise and fall of the tide and also by each species tolerance for conditions such as temperature, salinity, dessication etc. Many of the animals on the rock shore are fixed and unable to move away when, for example, the sunlight becomes too strong.

Tidal movement originates far above the shore: as the moon circles the earth, it exerts a "pull", causing the ocean to "bulge" in some places, and consequently, shrink in others. This pull is strongest when the sun, earth and moon are aligned and we have a full or a new moon. This, along with the earth's spin, creates the effect we know as a "spring tide" — the tide "comes in" to the highest level and "goes out" to the lowest, exposing the greatest amounts of seaweed. An ideal time for foraging. A week or so later, the tidal reach is much narrower when the moon and sun are at right angles to the earth. This is known as a neap tide, and it accompanies a half-moon. It takes just over six hours for tides to rise and fall in this part of the world, and thus we get two high tides and two low tides, roughly speaking, in every 24-hour period.

As the moon circles the earth, spring tides (extra high) occur twice every month and neap tides (extra low) also occur twice, on alternate weeks. As the earth circles the sun another pattern is created: on the equinoxes (March 21st and September 21st approximately) the spring and neap tides become extra high and low, and the opposite occurs at the solstices (June 21st and December 21st).

Zonation is easily visible on some taller rocks, where a colour pattern of black and orange defines where different lichen species live: Grey lichens grow at the highest level, well clear of salt water; Orange -yellow (*Xanthoria*) species flourish high on the rocks where they can tolerate sea spray and black (*Verrucharia*-type) lichens, with greatest tolerance for salt water, occupy the area just above high tide mark.

The tiny, rough, pale-grey shells often covering the rocks are barnacles, filter-feeders that draw nutrients from sea water when the tide comes in. Look closely at the overlapping plates on each one, making them robust and strong enough to withstand being stepped on. Limpets are the larger, conical shell gastropods attached to rocks, by a strong muscular sucker foot. They graze on seaweeds and other algae moving around to feed when the tide comes in.

Periwinkles have a single whorled shell and are grazers of brown seaweeds. Dog whelks and colourful topshells can be found hiding under seaweed and in crevices. Mussels usually grow on rocks where they filter plankton from seawater. Tiny blue-rayed limpets can be found attached to seaweed. The jelly-like, red beadlet anemone is firmly attached to rocks, hidden in crevices and ready to feed from the water with its stinging tentacles when the tide comes in.

Other factors are at play to create the differences we see on rocky shores. Some shores are exposed to wind and wave, others are more sheltered, such as coves and estuaries. This partly determines which species are present: alaria likes exposed shores, whereas some of the wracks like shelter. Seaweeds grow differently too — stunted , tougher versions may be found in more exposed areas. Barnacles and limpets both favour exposed shores, where their streamlined shape and wide base enables them to attach firmly to rocks. Mussels grow in tight clusters and high numbers on exposed shores, protecting each other, but they tend to grow much bigger on sheltered shores. The large brown kelps and wracks protect crabs on sheltered shores, protecting them from dessication or predation by birds such as oystercatchers and gulls.

As in all natural habitats, complex food webs exist on the shore, as do predator-prey relationships. Seabirds eat mussels, which in turn feed on plankton; fish feed on invertebrates; sea urchins eat limpets; limpets eat young seaweed; starfish eat mussels; sea mats live on seaweed; dog whelks eat periwinkles, which graze on seaweed; sea slugs feed on barnacles, which filter plankton from seawater and so on. Many species on the shore, whether carnivores or herbivores, ultimately depend on the seaweed, in the same way that the fauna of the land depend on green plants and trees. That is why a sustainable approach to foraging is recommended in this book.

So where does the rocky shore begin, or end? Not easy to answer, because although essentially a marine habitat, the shore is a transitional area between land and sea, and the boundaries are often gradual rather than well-defined. The co-existence of so many different life forms in such a narrow space, with quite extreme and changing conditions, is the outcome of millennia of evolution. It is a truly remarkable example of co-existence and survival of the fittest.

Our role as foragers in the rocky shore ecosystem brings with it a responsibility to nature: to limit our impact, to take only what's necessary, to remove all creatures from seaweed and place on rock or in seawater, to return stones and seaweed to their position, to minimise trampling and to leave nothing behind.

There are over nine thousand species of seaweed around the world. Ireland has over four hundred. Scientific research into seaweeds (their biology, nutritional and health value, commercial applications etc.) takes place at several irish and foreign universities and institutes. Currently, most of Ireland's commercial seaweed is used in agricultural food and fertilisers and in industrial applications. Some is used in cosmetics and a small proportion is commercially harvested for human consumption.

The Irish Wildlife Trust, a national, volunteer-based eNGO, has celebrated UN World Oceans Day for over a decade now, first on Howth Pier in Dublin and in 2004-2006, on Tramore beach in Co. Wateford. Using innovative touch pools and displays, games and guided walks, hundreds of children and adults were able to view the rocky shore habitat up close with volunteer rocky shore specialists, Tim Clabon and Catherine McCarney. For many, the revelation of the wonders of rock pools and the shore stimulated a life-long interest in learning more about this "Cinderella" of the natural world and about nature in general. IWT carried out a survey of the Honeycomb Worm (*Sabellaria*) reefs at Tramore in 2004, and highlighted the sensitivity of this protected species to trampling and water quality.

World Oceans Festival Tramore spawned the Oceanics Surf and Sea Festival, an annual celebration of the sea, held every September since 2008. An IWT outing on Kilfarassey strand in 2007, with some seaweed tasting thrown in, was a success, and it seemed people wanted to know more about seaweed, cooking, and rock pool ecology in general. The outing became a workshop, run by the author, along with IWT colleagues. It has been part of the Dungarvan Food Festival since 2008 and was recorded on RTE radio's Countrywide programme in 2010. Meeting people with an interest in seaweed, sharing tips and experimenting with new ways of using the "vegetables of the sea" evolved into the idea of writing it all down. Now the workshops take place across the region with cookery demonstrations, health benefits, and other uses of seaweeds. More information is available at www.theseagardener.ie.

Seaweed has been used on the land in Ireland for generations. It is particularly associated with potato growing, where it acts as a soil improver on light, sandy soils. There is a long tradition along the Co. Waterford coast of its use in this way. The potato growers of Ballinacourty achieved great success using seaweed gathered after storms on Clonea Strand.

Seaweed contains nutrients and trace elements, is lower in phosphates than farmyard manure, but higher in potash. Other properties ascribed to seaweed include plant health promotion, anti-fungal, plant growth promotion, increased resistance to frost damage, slug repellent, does not spread land plant diseases or weeds, germination catalyst, chelated micro-nutrients, quick decomposition due to low levels of cellulose and more. The anecdotal evidence for these claims is stronger than the scientific research at this time.

Gather only seaweed washed up on the strand (ideally following a storm) for gardening, as it is already dead. Even as it decomposes, seaweed provides shelter and nourishment for other living things, so only take what is necessary. Check with the local authority as removal of beach material may be subject to bye-laws in some areas.

- Add a layer to the compost bin to activate / speed up decomposition
- Use as a mulch around vegetables
- Make a liquid feed by adding the same volume of water to a bundle of seaweed and allow to stand for 8 weeks. Stir occasionally. Dilute the decanted liquid 1:30 with fresh water and apply to the soil around plants.
- Dig into the soil as with farmyard manure, if you have sandy soil.
- Especially good for potatoes and brassicas.
- Rinse with fresh water before using (as worms don't like high levels of salt), unless there has been a lot of rainfall to do it naturally.
- Check the legal position for its removal from beach with your local authority.
- Don't gather from polluted beaches.
- It has a strong smell, especially the liquid feed, and does attract flies so needs considerate use in confined gardens.
- Take only what you need – dead seaweed plays an important role in the decomposition cycle of nature on the beach.

MARIE POWER MEd, MIITD

Marie Power grew up on the Waterford Coast, and was given seaweed from an early stage because it was considered "good for you". She first learned how to cook in her mother Cait's kitchen. In her family, Paddy O'Reilly of Fenor and Jackie Power of Stradbally both believed in the benefits of dilisk, sleabhcan and carrageen. Her interest in seaweed as a tasty and nutritious addition to food was re-activated when she attended Prannie Rhatigan's Workshop in Annestown in 2007. Since then, she has been foraging and experimenting with different ways of using this novel food. Shore ecology was a key aspect of the World Oceans Festival she intiated on behalf of the Irish Wildlife Trust in Tramore in 2004. She now combines both passions and runs seaweed foraging workshops and cookery demonstrations for interested groups and schools.

www.theseagardener.ie

The Sea Garden